This book belongs to

_____

MENU

This book is dedicated to my children - Mikey, Kobe, and Jojo.

Ray Kroc

By Mary Nhin

Pictures By
Yuliia Zolotova

Hi, I'm Ray Kroc.

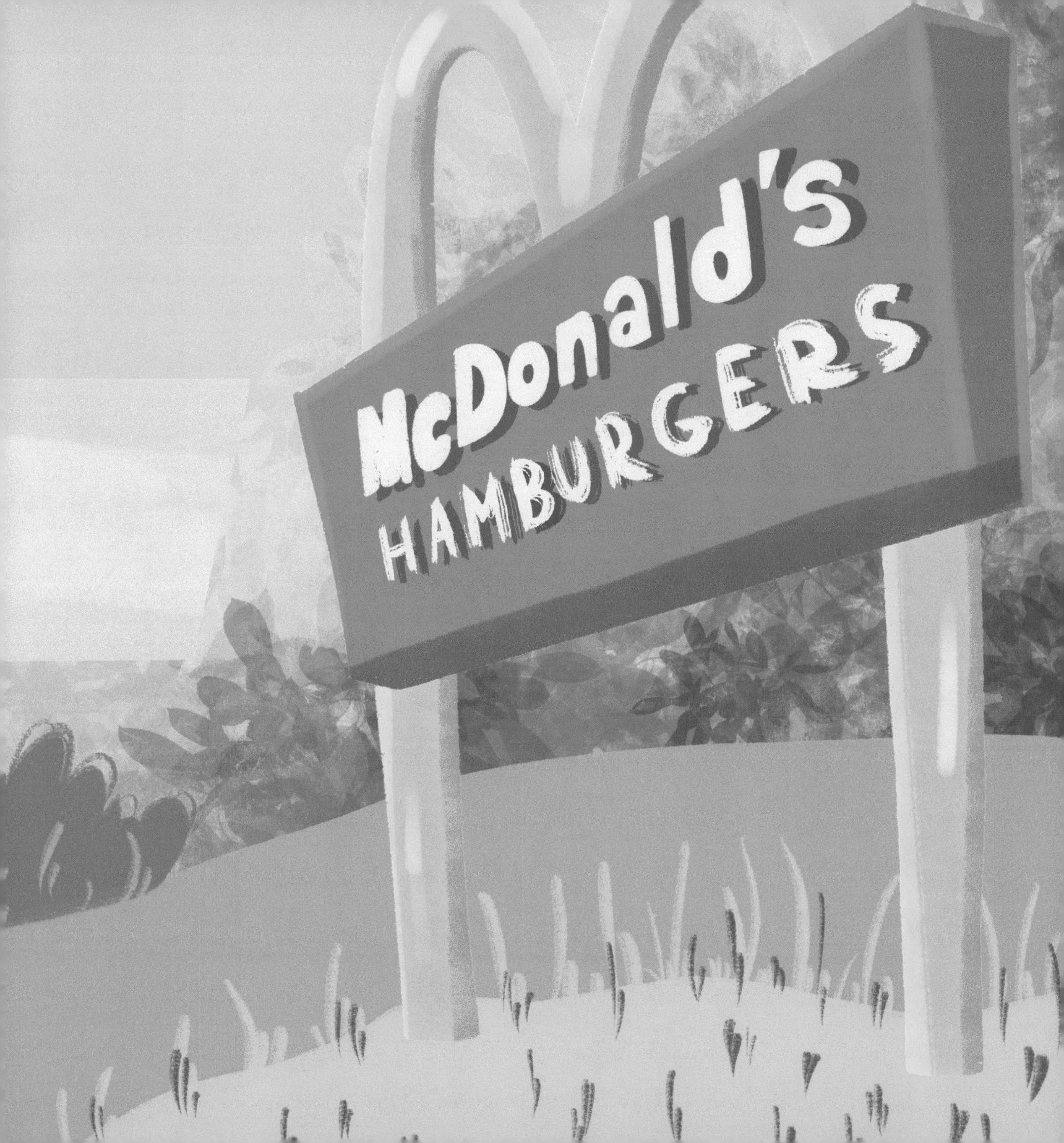
McDonald's
HAMBURGERS

Even as a child, I liked business. I was hard working and always looking for my next chance to make some money.

I tried lots of different jobs. I sold everything from houses to paper cups! I was used to handling rejection, and this built my persistence.

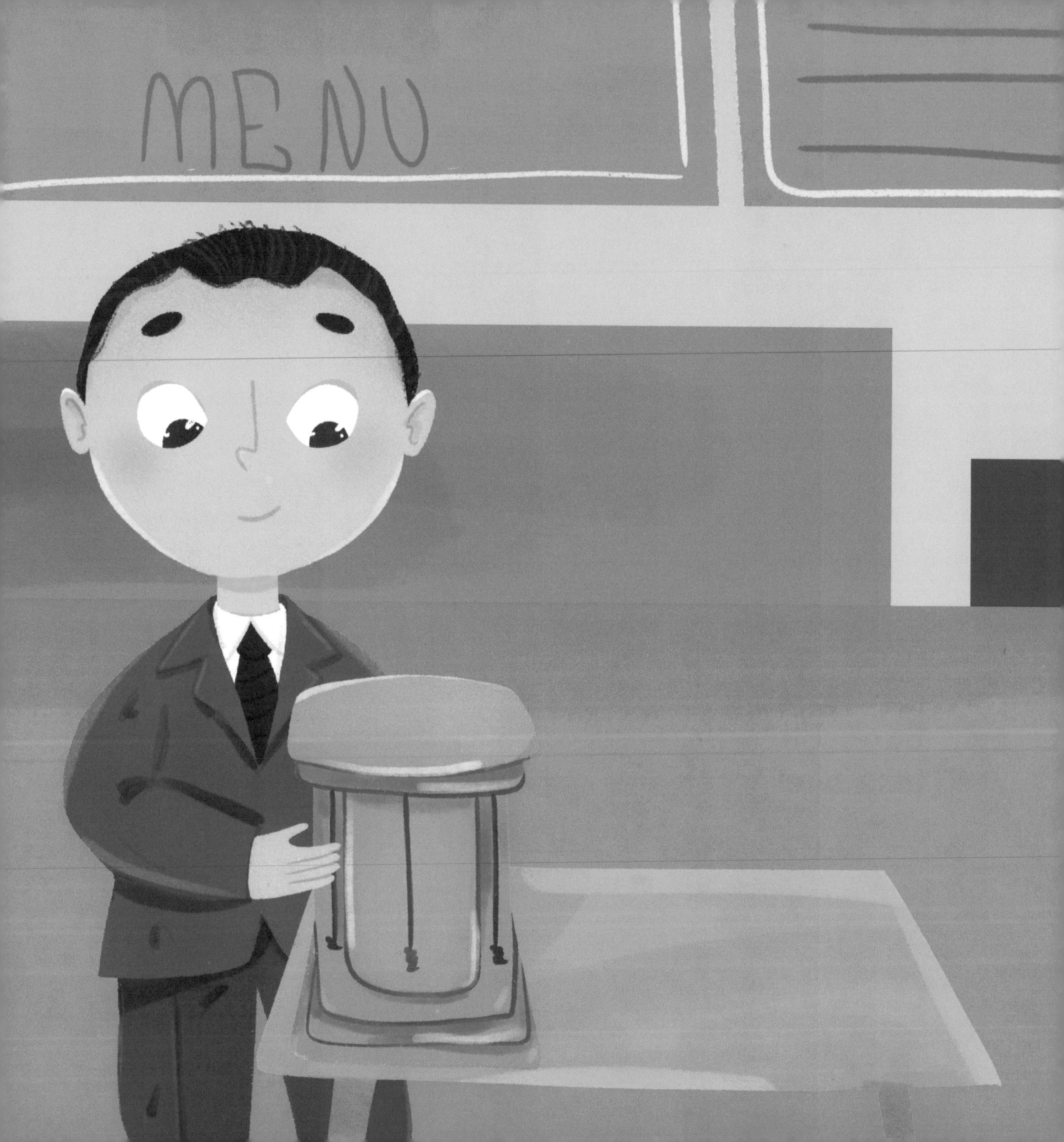
MENU

When I came across my big break, I was working at a job selling milkshake machines. To make sales, I visited many different diners and restaurants around America, trying to persuade the owners to buy a milkshake maker.

I got very used to seeing how the different restaurants in the U.S. all worked. Then one day on a trip to deliver some milkshake mixers, I visited a restaurant that was very different from all the others.

The restaurant was called McDonald's, and it was cleaner and friendlier than all the places I'd seen before.

The food came out quick and tasted great, too!

I soon became a McDonald's franchise agent. I envisioned a McDonald's in every American suburb. I tried to persuade the owners to let me expand the business by opening even more McDonald's restaurants in other towns and cities, but they didn't want to expand so much and as fast as I had hoped. But, I persisted.

I saw an opportunity in McDonald's so I asked the brothers if I could buy them out, and they agreed to sell for $2.7 million.

Finally, I was able to expand the franchise nationally without limitations from the original founders.

Expanding a restaurant had been done a lot of times before, but I had an idea to make it even better. I kept enough control of every restaurant to make sure that they were all very alike. The branding, the food, the furniture, the prices, everything had to be the same so that people always knew what to expect, no matter which McDonald's they visited.

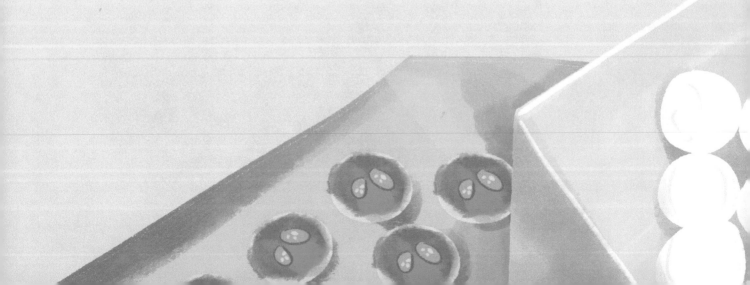

This made us reliable, and customers knew they could trust us which meant that they would come back to eat with us again.

We opened hundreds of McDonald's restaurants across America, and then expanded into other countries, too. I earned us a lot of money and became chief of one of the most successful restaurants in American history without ever having to learn how to cook!

Today, McDonald's is the world's largest restaurant chain by sales revenue and serves over 69 million customers daily in over 100 countries.

Timeline

1954 – Ray visits his first McDonald's while delivering milkshake machines

1961 – Ray becomes the owner of the company, McDonald's

1967 – Ray's company opens its first restaurants outside of the US, taking McDonald's international

1973 – Ray is awarded the Golden Plate Award by the American Academy of Achievement

2020 – McDonald's has nearly 40,000 restaurants around the world in over 100 different countries